fantastic FRAMES

Over 60 unique framing ideas

CREATIVE
PUBLISHING
international

MINNETONKA, MINNESOTA

Copyright © 1999
Creative Publishing international, Inc.
5900 Green Oak Drive
Minnetonka, Minnesota 55343
1-800-328-3895

President: Iain Macfarlane
Group Director, Book Development: Zoe Graul
Director, Creative Development: Lisa Rosenthal
Executive Managing Editor: Elaine Perry

Created by: The Editors of
Creative Publishing international, Inc.
Printed on American paper by:
R. R. Donnelley & Sons Co.
02 01 00 99/ 5 4 3 2 1

Library of Congress Cataloging-in-Publication Data

Fantastic frames.
    p. cm.
    Includes index.
    ISBN 0-86573-418-6 (soft cover)
    1. Picture frames and framing. I. Creative Publishing
International.
   N8550.F36 1999
   749'.7--dc21   98-49400

CONTENTS

Fantastic Frames 5

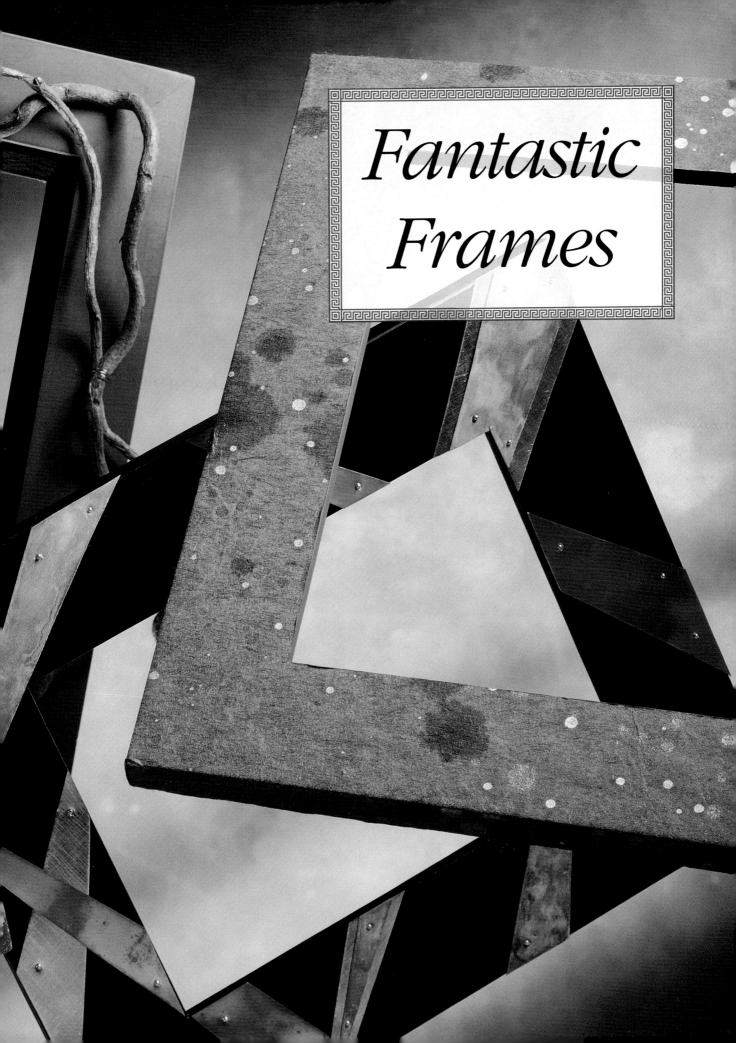

Fantastic Frames

DECORATIVE FRAMES

Starting with simple frames for pictures or mirrors, you can create frames that are eye-catching conversation pieces. A mix of several frames in various styles can be grouped together for added impact.

For a rustic, woodland look, make twig frames (top left). Or use your creativity to add moss, stones, or other natural materials (pages 26 and 27).

Embellished frames (far left) are quick and easy to make. Any number of items can be glued to frames, including buttons, coins, gemstones, beads, or charms.

Use a glue that will bond to both the frame and the embellishment. Hot glue is suitable for many items, including plastics, twigs, and bark. When gluing metal items, use a glue suitable for metals, such as a jewelry glue. When applying moss, use a wood glue. Because there must be sufficient bonding surface between the frame and the embellishment, a frame with a flat surface usually works best.

Decoupage frames (near left), embellished with cutouts from gift-wrapping paper, can be made in designs from Victorian to whimsical. For a quick decoupage finish, use an aerosol glaze. For a thick gloss on frames, use a glaze formulated for a triple-thick, extra-thick, or deep-gloss finish.

7

HOW TO MAKE A TWIG FRAME

MATERIALS

- Frame with flat surface in a color that matches the twigs.
- Straight twigs that will fit closely together.
- Hot glue gun and glue sticks; utility scissors.

1 Plan twig placement; cut twigs to the desired lengths. Position twigs on frame, arranging them as necessary for a close fit.

2 Secure twigs to one side of frame, applying the hot glue to the twigs. Glue twigs starting at inner edge of frame and working toward outer edge. Continue securing twigs to complete all sides.

HOW TO MAKE AN EMBELLISHED FRAME

MATERIALS

- Frame.
- Wire cutter.
- Embellishments, such as charms, shells, beads, buttons, and coins.
- Glue, appropriate for securing embellishments.

1 Remove any unnecessary hardware, such as button shanks or charm loops, from embellishments, using a wire cutter.

2 Plan placement of the items; for visual interest, consider using an asymmetrical design or extending some items over edge of frame.

3 Secure items with glue; to avoid excess glue, apply it sparingly to back of charm, making sure to cover all flat surfaces that will be in contact with frame.

HOW TO MAKE A DECOUPAGE FRAME

MATERIALS

- Frame.
- Gift-wrapping paper.
- Decoupage medium.
- Small sponge applicator, optional.
- Scissors with fine, sharp blades and points; curved cuticle scissors, for intricate, curved motifs.
- Spray glaze.

1 Cut out desired motifs from wrapping paper; if using cuticle scissors, cut with curved blades of scissors away from the motif.

2 Plan the placement of the motifs. Apply a thin layer of decoupage medium to back of motif, using sponge applicator or finger; secure to frame, taking care not to tear paper. Wipe any excess decoupage medium from frame.

3 Secure other embellishments, such as faceted stones, taking care not to use excessive amount of decoupage medium; allow to dry overnight.

4 Elevate frame on a piece of scrap wood or a jar. Apply several coats of spray glaze, allowing the glaze to dry between coats.

Give a whimsical look to a plain frame by applying simple motifs cut from copper or tin. Embellish the motifs to produce a variety of textures, including embossed, oxidized, and brushed. Nails, decorative tacks, or glue can be used to secure the metal accents to the frame.

Small copper and tin sheets and metal foils for embossing are available at craft stores and mail order suppliers. Copper is the thinner of the two metals, and it can be cut easily with household utility scissors. Tin can be cut best with jeweler's snips, available at jewelry-making supply stores.

HOW TO EMBELLISH A FRAME WITH METAL ACCENTS

MATERIALS

- Wooden frame.
- Copper or tin sheets, or 36-gauge metal foil, for embossed design.
- Utility scissors or jeweler's snips.
- Transfer paper, optional, for transferring embossing design.
- Scrap of wood.
- 100-grit sandpaper; 0000 steel wool.
- Tongs with handles that do not conduct heat, for oxidizing copper.
- 60-grit sandpaper, for brushed metal.
- Hammer and scrap of corrugated cardboard, for hammered effect.
- Patina solution, for antique verdigris finish on copper.
- Glue, or nails or decorative tacks.
- Aerosol clear acrylic sealer.

1 Mark outline of metal accent on metal sheet or foil. Embellish the metal foil with an embossed design, if desired (opposite).

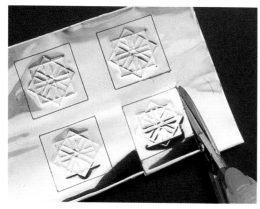

2 Cut on the marked lines, using scissors or jeweler's snips. Trim tips off any sharp points.

3 Place metal accents right side up over a scrap of wood. Using an awl, punch holes where nails or tacks will be used to secure the accents to the frame.

4 Sand edges of metal accents, using sandpaper to smooth any sharp edges of metal; avoid sanding surface of design if smooth finish is desired. Buff surface of metal, using steel wool. Embellish the metal accents with an oxidized, brushed, hammered, or antiqued finish as desired (opposite).

5 Apply several light coats of aerosol clear acrylic sealer to metal accents. Secure the metal accents to the frame, using nails, tacks, or glue. Predrill holes, using drill bit slightly smaller than nails or tacks.

TIPS FOR EMBELLISHING METAL

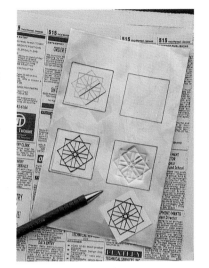

Embossed. Place metal foil on several layers of newspaper. Draw or trace the desired embossing design on paper. For an asymmetrical design, reverse the design. Tape the embossing design to the metal sheet. Using a pen with a ball point, trace along the design lines; retrace lines as necessary for desired detail.

Oxidized copper. Hold copper accent over flame, using tongs. Remove from heat and check color occasionally; holding copper in flame too long causes copper to lose all of its natural color.

Brushed surface. Texturize copper or tin by sanding metal lightly.

Verdigris finish. Apply chemical solution for reproducing antique verdigris finish to copper, following manufacturer's directions.

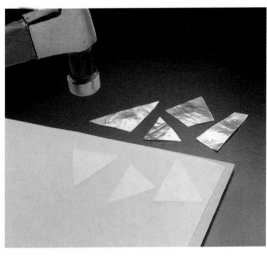

Hammered effect. Place copper or tin accent on a piece of corrugated cardboard, and cover with sheet of paper. Using a hammer, pound the copper for desired effect. Repeat on the back side.

FRAMES WITH DECORATIVE BUNDLES

Accent frames with bundles of natural materials, such as dried flowers, twigs, or rolls of handmade paper. Copper or brass wire is used to hold the bundles together; then, to secure the bundles in place, the wire ends arc laced through holes drilled into the frame. For best results, select a frame with a wide, flat surface. If you are using a frame with a preassembled back, be sure the drilled holes will not interfere with the backing of the frame.

HOW TO ADD DECORATIVE BUNDLES TO A FRAME

MATERIALS

- Wooden picture frame.
- 24-gauge or 28-gauge copper or brass craft wire.
- Natural materials as desired for bundles.
  - Drill and 1/16" drill bit.

1 Assemble bundles. Wrap each bundle several times with wire; twist wire on the back side, leaving about 4" (10 cm) excess wire at ends for securing bundle to frame.

2 Arrange the bundles as desired on the frame; using a pencil, mark the location for the holes, marking two dots about 1/4" (6 mm) apart for each bundle. Drill holes at the marked dots, using a 1/16" drill bit.

3 Insert the wire ends of bundle through holes; twist ends tightly behind the frame to secure bundle. Repeat for the remaining bundles. Trim excess wire.

PAPER-COVERED FRAMES

Give a new look to an old frame by covering it with decorative paper. Add other embellishments as desired, such as decorative tacks or paper cutouts.

Art supply stores carry papers in a variety of textures and colors, including corrugated paper and papers with grasses and fiber strands embedded in them. For best results, choose medium to heavyweight papers, because the tape that secures the paper to the frame may show through translucent papers. To protect the paper, display the frames away from direct sunlight.

HOW TO COVER A FRAME WITH PAPER

MATERIALS

- Picture frame with flat surface.
  - Decorative paper.
  - Double-stick transfer tape, or ATG tape.
  - Paint, for inside edges of frame, optional.
  - Decorative tacks, drill and ¹⁄₁₆" drill bit, optional.

1 Paint the inside edges of the frame opening, if desired; inside edges are covered with paper. Place the frame facedown over wrong side of paper; mark along the outer edges and the inner opening of frame. Measure the thickness of the frame. Mark lines on paper, adding this measurement to outer marked lines.

2 Cut along inner and outer marked lines, using a straightedge and a utility knife or a rotary cutter; for heavy papers, cut slightly outside the marked lines to allow for fold. Extend inner lines to outer lines at the corners; cut out corner squares as shown. Apply double-stick transfer tape to face of frame along inner and outer edges.

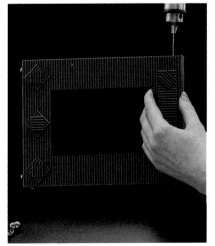

3 Center the frame over the back side of paper; press in place. Score heavy papers with a dull table knife along outer edges of frame. Apply double-stick transfer tape to sides of frame; wrap paper over the sides, and press paper in place.

4 Apply embellishments, if desired, securing with glue or tacks; if using tacks, predrill the holes, using a ¹⁄₁₆" drill bit, to prevent splitting hardwood frames.

MARBLEIZED FRAMES

The subtle and
elegant colors
of these marbleized
frames are easy to produce
using aerosol enamel paints. Paint
is floated in water; then the frame is
dipped into the water to pick up the color
randomly. The process can be repeated with
multiple colors to produce a frame with a mottled,
textural effect.

This technique can be used on flat-surfaced or dimensional
frames. Since no two marbleized frames are alike, this technique
is especially attractive for frames that are grouped together.

HOW TO MAKE A MARBLEIZED FRAME

MATERIALS

- Picture frame.
- Oil-based aerosol enamel paints, for base coat and marbleizing.
- Shallow pan larger than frame, such as a disposable aluminum pan.
- Disposable rubber gloves.

1 Apply base coat to the frame in desired color; allow to dry. Place water into pan to a depth of about 1" (2.5 cm). Spray paint over surface of water.

2 Dip face side of frame into water to coat front and sides with paint; take care to hold frame parallel to surface of water. Remove frame immediately.

3 Skim surface of water with piece of folded newspaper to remove excess paint. Repeat marbleizing process as desired for any remaining paint colors.

DUPLICATING AGED FINISHES

W hen you are shopping at antique stores, salvage yards, or garage sales, you will often find items that have wonderful detailing, but the finishes lack character or interest. The paint may be slightly chipped but not worn to the extent that you would like. Or someone may have even applied a fresh coat of paint to a wonderful old item, but you were looking for a piece that was weathered or worn.

Although you may prefer the authenticity of finishes that have aged on their own, aged finishes can be duplicated quite realistically. By duplicating an aged finish, you can select an old item for its style and detailing, rather than discounting it because the finish is not what you hoped for. In addition to the aged finishes shown here, the gold-leaf finish found on expensive antique picture frames and sconces can also be duplicated (page 22).

Before using any of the finishes, test the technique on a hidden area or on a scrap of a similar material, to become familiar with the process and to determine the effect you want to achieve.

Distressed wood, or the nicks and indentations in the wood on many old items, also contributes to the aged effect. If the piece you have is not as distressed as you would like it to be, you may distress the wood yourself before applying a finish.

Scrubbed finish is duplicated by removing the paint with a wire brush or sandpaper and applying beeswax for a subtle sheen.

Rusted finish is duplicated by painting the item black and then applying burnt sienna paint with a sea sponge.

Weathered finish is duplicated by applying paint to the item, allowing it to partially dry, and then removing some of it under running water.

Verdigris finish is duplicated by painting the item black and then applying aqua paint with a sea sponge.

Crackled finish is duplicated by applying a base coat of paint, a crackle medium, and a contrasting top coat of paint. Crackle medium makes the top coat crackle.

Worn finish is duplicated by applying paint to the item and then wiping it with a dampened rag to remove the paint in the areas that are normally subjected to wear.

GOLD-LEAF FINISH WITH AN AGED LOOK

A gold-leaf finish with an aged look gives found objects with intricate carved or raised detailing a rich, Old World effect. With its timeless, mellow look, this finish is often used for the picture frames of fine artwork found in museums. Because it may be used on wood, plaster, or cast-resin furnishings, it is also suitable for sconces, candlesticks, and small pieces of furniture. Although the finish requires several steps, the process is easy and the results are exquisite.

For this finish, use imitation gold leaf, sold in craft and art stores. For the dimensional effect, various materials are used in addition to the gold leaf, creating layers and depth. First, a base coat of paint is applied. Then the gold leaf is applied, followed by a clear acrylic sealer that protects the gold leaf from tarnishing. Because the gold leaf is almost translucent, the color of the base coat contributes to the color of the gold leaf. A red base coat, for example, gives a warm, rich gold finish while a white or gold base coat results in a lighter, brighter finish.

The remaining steps are designed to give the worn, Old World look to the finish. A heavy coat of latex or acrylic paint in taupe or cream is applied, then wiped away before it dries, except in the crevices and recessed areas. This is followed by a dusting of rottenstone powder, available at hardware stores, to add texture and aging to the gold-leaf finish.

MATERIALS

- Imitation gold leaf; water-based gold-leaf adhesive.
- Latex or acrylic paint in red or gold, for the base coat.
- Latex or acrylic paint in taupe, beige, or cream, for the top coat.
- Polyvinyl acrylic primer, if item is plaster.
- Rottenstone powder.
- Aerosol clear acrylic sealer.
- Paintbrushes, for applying paint, gold-leaf adhesive, and rottenstone powder; clean, lint-free rags; terry-cloth towel.

Gold-leaf finish may vary, depending on the paint colors used in the process, as you can see in these close-up details. The sconce (near right) has a red base coat under the gold leaf, with a beige top coat. The frame (far right) has a base coat of gold paint under the gold leaf, with a cream top coat.

HOW TO APPLY A GOLD-LEAF FINISH WITH AN AGED LOOK

1 Clean the found object as necessary. Apply a base coat of red or gold paint; allow to dry. If the item is plaster, apply a polyvinyl acrylic primer before applying the base coat.

2 Apply an even, light coat of gold-leaf adhesive, using paintbrush. Allow to set until clear, about one hour; surface will be tacky, but not wet.

3 Cut sheet of imitation gold leaf into smaller, manageable pieces, using scissors. Hold the gold leaf between the supplied tissues; avoid touching it directly with your hands. Slide the bottom tissue from underneath the gold leaf. Touching the top tissue, press gold leaf in place over the adhesive.

4 Remove top tissue. Using soft, dry paintbrush in an up-and-down motion, gently tamp the gold leaf in place to affix it. Then smooth gold leaf, using brush strokes.

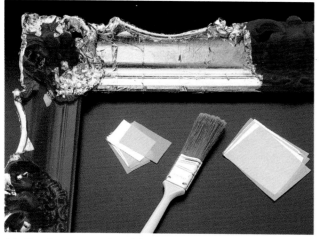

5 Continue to apply additional pieces of the gold leaf, overlapping them slightly; the excess gold leaf at the edges will brush away.

6 Fill in any gaps between sheets of gold leaf as desired by applying adhesive and scraps of gold leaf. Apply two coats of aerosol clear acrylic sealer; allow to dry.

7 Apply a heavy coat of latex or acrylic paint in a burnt umber, taupe, beige, or cream, over the gold leafing. On large project, work on one section at a time, applying the paint and completing step 8 before moving on to the next section.

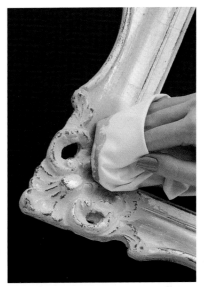

8 Allow paint to partially dry; when paint begins to set, wipe paint off with a clean, lint-free rag. Start by applying light pressure, and then rubbing harder, if necessary. Remove most of the paint in the smooth areas, leaving paint in the carved areas, the crevices, and corners. If paint is difficult to remove, a slightly damp rag may be used.

9 Sprinkle a generous amount of rottenstone powder over the entire project while paint is still slightly damp. Tamp the powder down, using a paintbrush.

10 Leave rottenstone powder on project for 20 minutes; then remove the excess powder with a soft-bristle paintbrush.

11 Buff the raised areas and edges very hard, using terry-cloth towel. Base coat should show in some areas, for a worn effect.

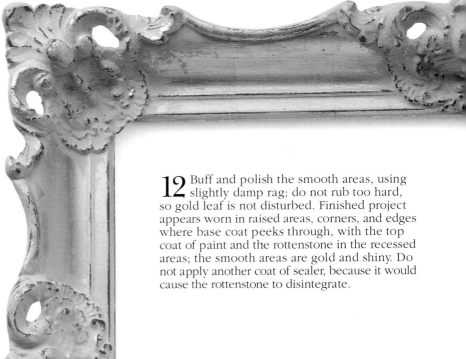

12 Buff and polish the smooth areas, using slightly damp rag; do not rub too hard, so gold leaf is not disturbed. Finished project appears worn in raised areas, corners, and edges where base coat peeks through, with the top coat of paint and the rottenstone in the recessed areas; the smooth areas are gold and shiny. Do not apply another coat of sealer, because it would cause the rottenstone to disintegrate.

MORE IDEAS
FOR DECORATIVE FRAMES

Spanish moss and twigs *embellish a mirror with a simple, wide frame.*

Bundled twigs, *tied with raffia, make a woodland frame.*

Buttons and beads *are tied at the corner of a rustic frame. A hole drilled through the frame allows for lacing the items.*

Polished stones are glued to a frame to complement a nature print.

Gift card is cut to make a decorative mat. Use a straightedge and a mat knife to cut an opening for the picture.

MORE IDEAS FOR DECORATIVE FRAMES
(CONTINUED)

Curly willow *adds drama and texture to a framed mirror. The curly willow is secured with 16-gauge wire nails; to prevent splitting the wood, predrill the holes, using a 1/16" drill bit. Copper charms are wired to the twigs for interest.*

Wired ribbon bow, *trimmed with a brass charm, embellishes the top of a traditional frame. Secure the bow and charm to the frame with hot glue.*

Painted wooden medallion, *secured with glue, adds a raised design to a simple frame. Before attaching the medallion, give the frame a marbleized finish as on page 18.*

Multicolored painted frame
enhances artwork. Paint the frame
in sections, masking off areas as
necessary, using tape.

Beads, secured to the edges of a frame with nails,
provide a colorful accent. Holes are predrilled into
the edges of the frame; then 16-gauge nails, threaded
with beads, are inserted into the holes and secured
in place with a dot of glue.

Brass knobs (right) serve as key hooks on a wide,
wooden frame. Predrill the holes for the knobs.

Stones and glass gems (below), selected
to complement the artwork, are secured to
a painted frame with hot glue.

FABRIC-COVERED PICTURE FRAMES

Create custom picture frames using fabrics that coordinate with your decorating scheme. Picture frames are an inexpensive way to introduce luxurious fabrics, such as silks, damasks, and tapestries. Embellish the frames, if desired, with trims, charms, or appliqués.

For best results, use firmly woven lightweight to mediumweight fabrics. If you are using a heavier fabric, reduce bulk by covering the frame back and the stand with a lightweight fabric. Lightly pad the frame, if desired, using polyester fleece.

- Fabric.
- Polyester fleece, optional.
- Heavy cardboard, such as mat board or illustration board; precut mats may be used for the frame front.
- Clear acetate sheet, optional.
- Fabric glue, diluted slightly with water for easier spreading.
- Flat paintbrush or sponge applicator for applying glue.
- Aerosol adhesive intended for fabric use.
- Hot glue gun and glue sticks.

CUTTING DIRECTIONS

Determine the desired size of the frame and the frame opening; the opening should be slightly smaller than the photograph or picture. Mark these dimensions on the cardboard for the frame front. Mark the frame back on the cardboard ½" (1.3 cm) narrower and shorter than the frame front. Make the frame stand, if desired, as on page 32, steps 1 and 2, cutting the pieces for the frame stand with a mat knife and a straightedge. When cutting with a mat knife, it is better to use a few medium-pressure cuts than one heavy cut. Cut a clear acetate sheet, if desired, to the size of the photograph or picture.

HOW TO MAKE A FABRIC PICTURE FRAME

1 Position the frame front on wrong side of fabric; trace around frame and opening, using a pencil or chalk. Cut fabric 1" (2.5 cm) outside marked lines. Position frame back on wrong side of fabric, and trace around it; cut 1" (2.5 cm) outside the marked lines. Trace a second back piece; cut ⅛" (3 mm) inside marked lines.

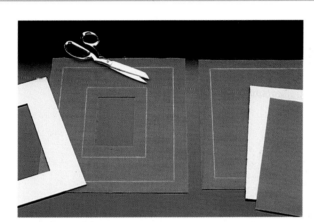

2 Apply fleece, if desired, to frame front, using aerosol adhesive; trim even with edges of cardboard.

3 Center frame front, fleece side down, on wrong side of the fabric for frame front; clip fabric at corners of frame opening to within a scant ⅛" (3 mm) of cardboard. Using diluted fabric glue, secure fabric to cardboard around the opening, gluing alternating sides.

4 Apply glue at one outer corner and along edges to center of adjacent sides. Wrap fabric firmly around edge of frame, pinching fabric together at corner as shown. Repeat for the remaining sides and corners.

5 Fold excess fabric at corners flat; secure with diluted fabric glue.

6 Apply smaller piece of fabric to frame back, using aerosol adhesive. Center frame back, fabric side up, on the wrong side of remaining fabric piece; secure with aerosol adhesive. Wrap and glue sides as for frame front. Seal raw edges of fabric with diluted fabric glue; this is inside of frame back.

(Continued)

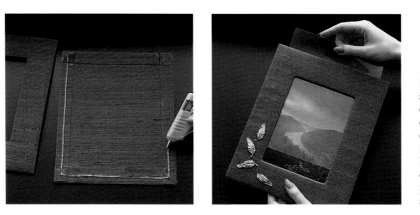

7 Apply hot glue to the inside of frame back along three edges; center the frame back on the frame front, and secure. One side of the frame is left open for inserting a photograph or a picture.

8 Make and attach frame stand (below), if desired. Attach embellishments as desired, securing them with glue. Insert photograph or picture and protective clear acetate sheet.

HOW TO MAKE A FRAME STAND

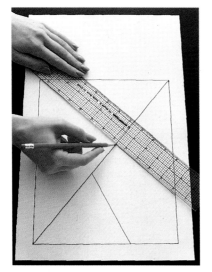

1 Mark the dimensions of frame on paper; divide rectangle in half diagonally. Measuring from the lower corner, mark point on each side of corner a distance equal to about one-third the width of the frame. Align a straightedge with one point and opposite corner; mark line from the point to diagonal marked line. Repeat for remaining point.

2 Cut out the frame stand pattern. Position on cardboard; trace. Cut out frame stand. Lightly score cardboard ½" (1.3 cm) from upper edge, using straightedge and mat knife; do not cut through cardboard. Flip stand over and gently crease cardboard along scored line as shown.

3 Position stand on wrong side of fabric, scored side up; trace. Cut ½" (1.3 cm) outside marked lines. Turn stand over and repeat to cut second piece, cutting ⅛" (3 mm) inside marked lines; this is lining piece.

4 Center stand, scored side up, on wrong side of larger fabric piece. Using diluted glue and brush, apply glue to the edges of fabric, and wrap around the edges of stand, clipping fabric at corners. Secure lining piece, centered, using aerosol adhesive. Seal the raw edges of fabric with diluted fabric glue.

5 Apply hot glue to lining side of frame stand above scored line. Secure the stand to the back of the frame, matching outer edges at the corner of the frame.

MORE IDEAS FOR PICTURE FRAMES

Brass wire *is wrapped around the corners of a fabric-covered frame for embellishment. The wire is applied before the back is secured in place.*

Wallcovering cutouts *embellish an acrylic frame. The wallcovering is applied using border adhesive.*

Wallcovering border *is used to trim a wooden frame.*

Trio of frames *is hinged by inserting ribbon between the frame fronts and backs. A ⅛" (3 mm) space is allowed between the frames to allow for folding. No frame stands are needed for hinged frames.*

COPPER FOIL
PICTURE FRAMES

Copper foil tape, available at stained glass supply stores, is used to make these quick and creative picture frames. The artwork or photograph is encased between mat board and glass and sealed at the edges with the copper foil tape. Pressure between layers keeps the artwork or photograph from sliding out of position.

The mat board may be used simply as a backing for the project when no margin is desired around the artwork or photograph, such as with children's paintings or classic advertising art. When a margin is desired, choose a mat board that will complement or set off the artwork or photograph; cut the glass and mat board larger to allow for the desired margin of mat board to show. As another alternative, use a second piece of glass for the backing instead of the mat board, thus allowing the artwork or photograph to seemingly float in air.

Glass can be cut to size at the store, or you can cut it yourself, following steps 1 to 6 on page 36. Safety glasses are recommended whenever you are cutting glass, to protect your eyes from flying glass splinters. Clean up the work surface with a hand broom after cutting glass; never brush the surface with your hand.

Adhesive hangers may be applied to the back of the framed project for hanging on the wall. For display on a shelf or table, the framed project may be supported on a plate stand or small easel.

HOW TO MAKE A COPPER FOIL PICTURE FRAME

MATERIALS

- Artwork or photograph to be framed.
- Single-strength glass and tools for cutting glass, as listed on page 36.
- Mat board.
- Mat knife.
- Binder clips.
- 3/8" (1 cm) or 1/2" (1.3 cm) copper foil tape.
- Wooden craft stick.
- Self-adhesive picture hanger, for hanging on wall.
- Plate stand or small easel, for free-standing display.

CUTTING DIRECTIONS

Cut the glass to the desired finished size, following steps 1 to 6 on pages 36 and 37. Cut one piece for a frame with mat board backing; cut two pieces for a frame with glass backing. For a frame with mat board backing, cut the mat board to the same size as the glass, using a mat knife.

Cut a length of foil tape to the exact measurement of each side of the glass.

1 Frame with mat board backing. Place artwork or photograph faceup on right side of mat board backing in desired position. Clean both sides of glass thoroughly; place glass over artwork or photograph, aligning edges to backing. Clamp the layers together, using binder clips.

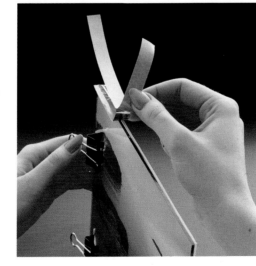

2 Peel about 2" (5 cm) of protective backing from one length of foil tape; remove the binder clips along corresponding side. Apply foil tape to outer edge, centering tape over backing and glass so equal amounts will wrap to the front and back. Continue to remove backing as tape is applied.

3 Fold edges of copper foil tape to front and back. Smooth edges of tape firmly, using wooden craft stick, to ease out any bubbles or gaps.

(Continued)

4 Repeat steps 2 and 3 for remaining sides, beginning with side opposite the first side. Attach self-adhesive picture hanger to back of frame, if desired.

Frame with glass backing. Follow steps 1 to 4 on pages 35 and 36, using glass backing instead of mat board. Mark placement of artwork on back side of glass backing, using narrow tape.

HOW TO CUT GLASS

MATERIALS

- Single-strength glass.
- Fine-tip marking pen; cork-backed straightedge.

- Glass cutter.
- Grozing pliers.

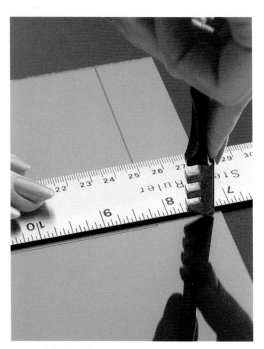

1 Mark cutting lines on glass, using fine-tip marking pen and cork-backed straightedge. Use outer edges of glass sheet as one or two sides whenever possible. Place straightedge along one marked line on glass, from one edge of glass sheet completely across to the opposite edge. Check to see that the wheel of the glass cutter (arrow) will line up exactly on marked line.

2 Hold the glass cutter perpendicular to the glass, with the wheel parallel to the straightedge, beginning ⅛" (3 mm) from one edge of the glass. Hold the straightedge firmly in place with the other hand.

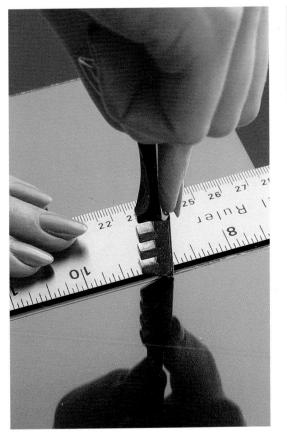

3 Push or pull the glass cutter, depending on which is more comfortable for you, across the glass from edge to edge, to score the glass; exert firm pressure, maintain constant speed, and keep the cutter perpendicular to the glass. Ease up on the pressure as you score off the glass on the opposite edge. Score the glass only once; do not repeat the process.

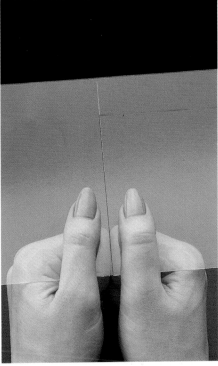

4 Hold the glass in both hands with the scored line between your thumbs; curl your fingers under the glass, making fists, with knuckles touching each other.

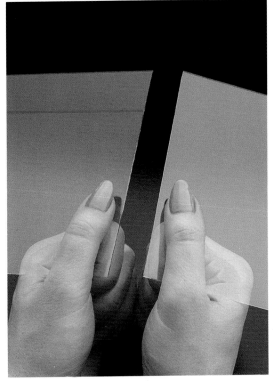

5 Apply quick, even pressure as you roll your thumbs out from each other, turning your wrists upward; this breaks the glass along the scored line.

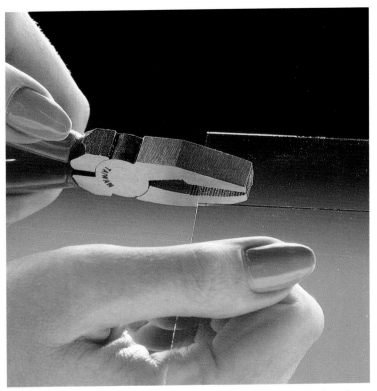

6 Repeat steps 2 to 5 for each remaining line marked on the glass. If the glass is not wide enough to grasp safely or effectively with your fingers, use grozing pliers, holding the pliers at a right angle close to the end of the score, with the flat jaw of the pliers on top of the glass.

Simple rustic frames, created from weathered wood and tree bark, blend well in a country setting or add a surprising touch to a contemporary room. Collect loose tree bark from firewood or fallen trees. If the bark is not loose, cut it lengthwise with a utility knife and pry the bark away from the wood with a wood chisel or putty knife. Scrape off any excess fibrous material from the back of the bark. Flatten slightly curled bark by steaming it with an iron and pressing it between two boards until dry. Moisten severely curled bark, and seal it in a plastic bag until it is pliable enough to press flat.

HOW TO MAKE A BARK FRAME

MATERIALS

- Tree bark.
- Utility knife.
- Photograph or artwork.
- Glass and tools for cutting glass, as listed on page 36.
- Foam board, 3/8" (1 cm) thick.
- Hot glue gun and glue sticks.
- Mat board.
- Embellishments, such as lichens or moss, if desired.
- Self-adhesive hanger, if desired.

CUTTING DIRECTIONS

Cut the bark to the desired size, using a utility knife, or tear the bark to the desired size and shape. Cut the glass (page 36) to the same size as the photograph. Cut three spacers from foam board, 1/2" (1.3 cm) wide, with the length of one spacer equal to the length of the lower edge of the glass and the length of the remaining two spacers equal to the length of the sides of the glass. Cut a mat board backing 1" (2.5 cm) longer than the sides of the glass and 1¾" (4.5 cm) wider than the upper and lower edges of the glass. Cut a mat board shim the same size as the photograph.

1 Place the bark frame facedown on work surface. Mark opening in desired location on the back of the frame, with measurements 1/2" (1.3 cm) narrower and shorter than the width and length of the glass and photograph. Cut opening, using utility knife.

2 Glue foam board spacer for lower edge of opening to back of frame, using hot glue gun and centering spacer 1/4" (6 mm) below opening. Glue the foam board spacers for the sides 3/8" (1 cm) beyond opening edges.

3 Glue the mat board backing over spacers; lower and side edges of the backing will extend 1/4" (6 mm) beyond spacers. Attach a self-adhesive hanger, if desired.

4 Place the photograph facedown on glass; place mat board shim over the photograph; slide into place between the backing and the frame opening. Embellish with lichens or moss, if desired, gluing them to bark.

HOW TO MAKE A WEATHERED WOOD FRAME

MATERIALS

- Weathered wood.
- Artwork or photograph to be mounted.
- Glass and tools for cutting glass, as listed on page 36.
- Mat board for backing.

- Decorative upholstery tacks.
- Tack hammer.
- Two sawtooth hangers.
- Embellishments, such as lichens or moss, if desired.
- Hot glue gun and glue sticks.

CUTTING DIRECTIONS

Cut the weathered wood, if necessary, to the desired size. Cut the glass (page 36) and mat board backing to the same size as the artwork.

1 Attach sawtooth hanger to each top upper corner on back of frame.

2 Stack mat board backing, artwork, and glass in desired location on weathered wood frame.

3 Nail two decorative upholstery tacks, evenly spaced along each side of stack, with shanks of tacks close to, but not touching, glass and underside of tack heads just above glass.

4 Embellish with lichens or moss, if desired, using hot glue gun.

MORE IDEAS
FOR FRAMES

Copper mounting plate with verdigris finish provides a backdrop for artwork encased in copper foil frame (page 35).

Scuff copper sheet with sandpaper. Apply verdigris finish, following manufacturer's instructions. Mount copper foil frame, using hot glue.

Mark the desired opening. Drill holes in four corners of marked opening, with large drill bit. Cut opening, using jigsaw; insert blade of jigsaw into drilled holes, and cut along marked lines

Weathered wood frame features rough-cut openings for photographs. Back of frame is constructed like bark frame on page 39.

LEATHER FRAMES

Make unique custom-sized picture frames by lacing three layers of leather together. Use a stiff leather for the frame backing and stand, to provide the proper support; a softer, lightweight leather or suede may be used for the frame front. If vegetable-tanned lather is used, the frames may be stained or personalized with stamped designs.

The leather skins and any necessary supplies are available at leather craft and supply stores. For lacing the edges of the frames, leather and suede lacing is available in various widths. To determine the amount of lacing needed, allow about four times the distance around the outside of the frame.

A punch tool and mallet are used to make lacing holes in leather quickly and easily. Punch tools are available in many sizes; a size 4, or 5/32" (3.8 mm), punch tool will work for most lacing. Saddle-stamping tools, available in a variety of designs, are used for making stamped designs on heavyweight vegetable-tanned leather. When punching and stamping leather, work on a hard, smooth surface, such as a sturdy workbench or a piece of firm Masonite® or marble.

For aligning stamped designs, a placement line may be lightly scored on the leather with your fingernail. Do not draw the line with a pencil, because pencil markings often cannot be removed without marring the leather. A pencil may be used for marking lacing holes that will be punched out of the leather.

Special leather stains are available in several shades. They not only change the color of a vegetable-tanned leather, they also bring out the grain and enhance any stamped designs. Before applying stain to a project, test it on a scrap of the leather you will be using. If stain is being applied to a lightweight leather, some shrinkage may occur. Leather finishes are also available; they provide a durable, water-repellent finish and a soft luster.

MATERIALS

- Leather.
- Leather lacing.
- Leather round-drive punch tool, in size appropriate for lacing; a size 4, or 5/32", will work for most leather lacing.
- Two-pronged leather-lacing needle.
- Mallet, of wood, rubber, or rawhide.
- Mat knife or rotary cutter; metal straightedge.
  - Cardboard, optional, for frame.
  - Saddle-stamping tools, for stamped designs.
  - Leather stain, optional.
  - Leather finish.

Leather picture frame gives a room the rustic look of a country lodge.

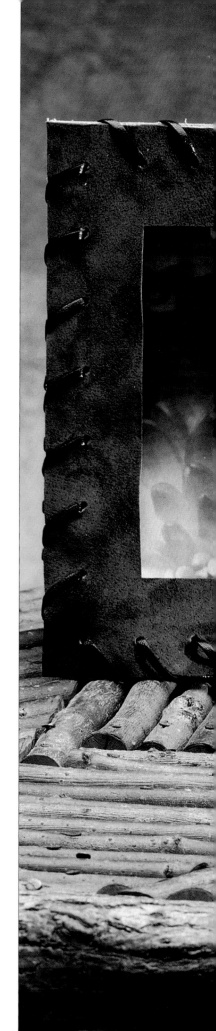

HOW TO MAKE A LACED LEATHER FRAME

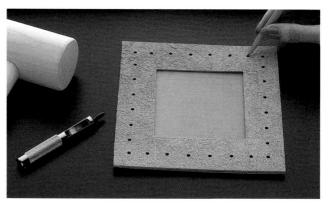

1 Determine size of picture opening; picture can be no more than ¼" (6 mm) wider than opening. To length and width, add 2¾" (7 cm) to allow for 1⅜" (3.5 cm) borders; this is finished size. Cut two pieces of stiff leather equal to the finished size, using mat knife; these will be frame back and stand. Cut a third piece for frame front; this may be cut from leather of a lighter weight. Mark picture opening on frame front; cut.

2 Mark placement for lacing holes on top side of frame front, ½" (1.3 cm) from edges, using pencil or chalk; position a hole at each corner and at regular intervals of about ¾" (2 cm). Punch holes, using a punch tool and a mallet. Place the frame front on the frame stand, top sides together. Using the frame front as a guide, mark holes on the frame stand. Punch holes.

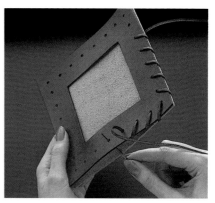

3 Mark and punch holes on frame back; at lower edge, punch only one hole in from each corner hole. This leaves opening for inserting picture. Stamp, stain, and finish the leather, if desired (opposite).

4 Position frame front on back, top sides facing out. Secure lacing to leather needle. Insert needle from back of frame, into hole about one-third the distance from the top; leave tail for knotting ends.

5 Lace the frame together, using whipstitch, along first side and lower edge; at opening on lower edge, lacing is done through frame front only.

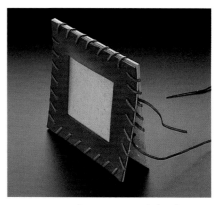

6 Lace the remaining side to hole opposite starting point. Position frame stand against frame back, with top sides facing out.

7 Lace through all layers of frame to attach stand to upper portion of sides and along top edge.

8 Continue lacing around the frame stand only.

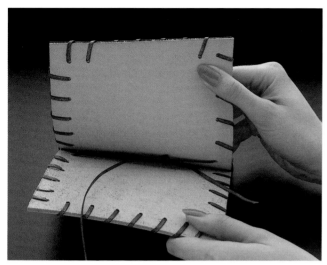

9 Bring ends of lacing across the frame, between frame back and frame stand; tie ends together. Trim tails.

10 Insert the picture into laced frame.

HOW TO STAMP, STAIN & FINISH LEATHER

1 Stamp. Prepare leather by wiping both sides with a dampened sponge; place in plastic bag, and allow to set several hours. Remove leather from bag; allow surface of leather to dry, just until original leather color returns.

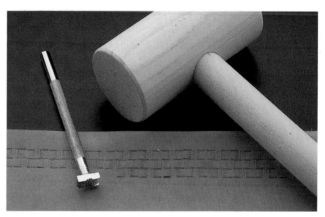

2 Place leather on hard, smooth surface, top side up. Position saddle-stamping tool on leather; pound with mallet until imprint is clear.

Stain. Stamp leather, if desired. Apply a liberal coat of leather stain to leather, using a rag and circular motion; allow to set several minutes. Remove excess stain, using a dampened sponge; if leather is stamped, stain should remain in crevices of stamped design. Allow to dry.

Finish. Apply an even, light coat of leather finish, using dampened sponge; allow to dry. Apply second coat of finish. When dry, buff leather with soft rag.

DISPLAYING OLD ARTWORK IN CLIP FRAMES

Clip frames are ideal for displaying old artwork or news clippings because the simplicity of the frames allows the artwork itself to show off. Clip frames work well for any decorating scheme, but especially for modern interiors. Essentially, each frame consists of a piece of glass with a tension-mounted backing board. Clip frames are available from craft stores, art stores, and framing supply stores.

To enhance the artwork, you may add creative touches like irregular hand stitches, woven lengths of raffia, or pressed flowers. As a background for the framed objects, use a sheet of mat board or art paper. Keep in mind that the available mounting depth is limited by the frame's mounting brackets. Therefore, if dimensional items are used for embellishments, avoid using mat board or other heavyweight paper for the background.

Clip frames, readily available at craft stores, art stores, and framing supply stores, are easily assembled. First, secure the artwork to a sheet of art paper or mat board. Then, lay the artwork and the backing board facedown on the glass, and slide the clips in place.

Old print *(below) is secured to a textured paper with hand stitches. Metallic thread is used.*

Old magazine advertisement (right) mounted on handmade paper makes an eye-catching piece of artwork.

Old family photographs (above) are arranged in a grouping with pressed flowers and a lace doily.

Old postcard (right) is mounted on rice paper with a cedar sprig and birch bark as accents.

Call for Life Savers...
say "hello" to refresh-mint!

...th the hole

PEP·O·MINT
LIFE SAVERS

still only 5¢

Greetings from the
REDWOODS

DISPLAYING ARTWORK ON CANVASES

Artist's canvases provide a quick and inexpensive way to display artwork such as photographs, postcards, and greeting cards. The white canvas serves as a mat. Pine lath, nailed around the edges of the canvas, becomes the frame.

Prestretched cotton canvases, stapled to a wooden frame, are available at art supply stores and craft stores and come in many sizes. Select the dimensions that will give the desired border width around the artwork.

The artwork is secured to the canvas with double-stick transfer tape, or ATG tape. For this reason, and because the artwork is not protected by glass, this mounting and display method is not recommended for artwork that is valuable.

MATERIALS

- Artist's prestretched cotton canvas.
- $\frac{1}{4}$" × $1\frac{3}{8}$" (6 mm × 3.5 cm) pine lath.
- Paint, or stain and matching putty, for pine lath.
- 16 × $\frac{3}{4}$" (2 cm) brads; nail set.
- Drill and $\frac{1}{16}$" drill bit.
- Double-stick transfer tape or ATG tape.
- Rubber bumpers; sawtooth picture hanger.

HOW TO DISPLAY ARTWORK USING AN ARTIST'S CANVAS

1 Cut pine lath to length of canvas top and bottom. Repeat for sides, adding $\frac{1}{2}$" (1.3 cm) to length of side lath strips to allow for overlap of lath at ends. Sand ends lightly; apply a paint or stain to lath strips.

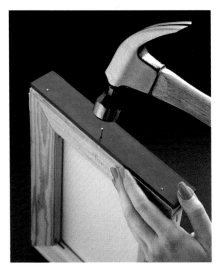

2 Align the top lath strip to wooden frame of stretched canvas, at the back edge and ends of frame. Secure with brads; predrill holes, and space the brads about 1" (2.5 cm) from the ends and at about 5" (12.5 cm) intervals. Repeat to secure bottom lath strip; then secure the side strips.

3 Secure each corner with a brad, predrilling holes. Countersink brads, using a nail set; fill holes with putty to match stain, or touch up with paint.

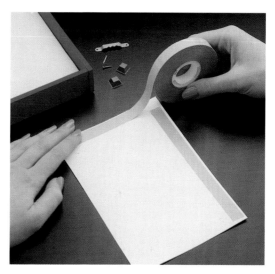

4 Apply double-stick transfer tape to back side of artwork along the outer edges; for larger pieces, apply one or more additional strips in the center area. Position artwork as desired on the canvas; press in place. Secure the sawtooth hanger to back of frame, centering at the upper edge. Secure rubber bumpers at lower corners.

MORE IDEAS FOR DISPLAYING ARTWORK

Empty frame, *propped against the wall, provides an opportunity to showcase three-dimensional star and moon forms. The framed objects are suspended from the frame with monofilament fishing line. The remaining items are secured to the wall with silicone glue.*

Weathered board *is the mounting surface for this nature picture. Narrow strips of leather, secured to the board with tacks, hold the image in place.*

Clipboards *(right), hung on the wall, allow children's artwork to be changed with ease. The clipboards are personalized with paint pens.*

Foam-core board is used as a background for dry-mounted prints. Dry-mounting is done professionally at custom framing shops.

Double layer of glass replaces the traditional frame assembly, allowing the wall to become the mat. This interesting technique, however, does not protect the artwork indefinitely.

FRAMED BOTANICALS

Pressed flowers and leaves can be mounted in prematted frames for a classic wall arrangement. The natural beauty of pressed flowers surpasses that of botanical prints, at a fraction of the cost.

Single large leaves or clusters of small pressed flowers and grasses can be arranged on rice paper for a textural background. Then cover the botanical materials with a sheet of extra-thin glass to hold them securely, and place the layers in a purchased frame.

MATERIALS

- Inexpensive frame with a precut mat.
- Extra-thin glass.
- Glass cutter.
- Rice paper.
- Pressed flowers, leaves, or grasses.
- Double-stick framer's tape or craft glue.
- Brads; split-joint pliers.

HOW TO MAKE FRAMED BOTANICALS

1 Remove the backing, precut mat, and glass from frame. Cut a piece of extra-thin glass, as on page 36, cutting it to same size as the glass provided with the frame. Clean both of the glass pieces thoroughly.

2 Cut rice paper to fit the backing provided with frame. Attach paper to backing at corners, using double-stick framer's tape or dots of glue.

3 Arrange pressed floral materials on the rice paper, checking to see that arrangement fits within mat opening.

4 Position extra-thin glass over pressed floral materials and rice paper. Position precut mat over extra-thin glass.

5 Position the original glass over precut mat and other layers; then position the frame over the glass.

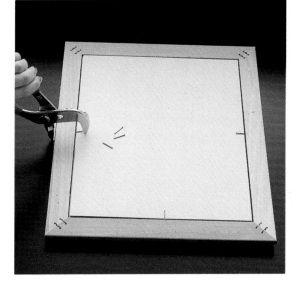

6 Turn frame over, keeping all layers firmly in place. Secure the layers into the frame, using small brads and split-joint pliers; pressure between layers keeps the flowers in place.

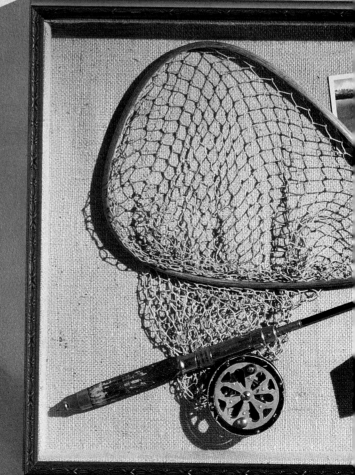

Shadow boxes (above and right) display cherished family memorabilia.

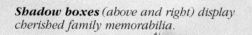

DISPLAYING
MEMORABILIA
IN SHADOW BOXES

Showcase cherished mementos of the past in shadow boxes. These frames have deep sides that allow you to mount dimensional items, such as jewelry, watches, and other memorabilia. Shadow boxes are available in many styles and finishes and can be ordered in the desired size and depth at framing shops.

Foam-core board, wrapped with fabric, is used for the mounting board and to line the sides of the frame. For conservation framing, use acid-free foam-core board and natural-fiber fabric, such as 100 percent silk, linen, or cotton.

To determine the shadow box size you need, arrange all the objects to be framed on a sheet of craft paper, making sure to allow the desired amount of space around each item. Mark the frame size, and outline the items on the paper to record the placement. To determine the frame depth, measure the deepest item; add ½" (1.3 cm) to this measurement to allow for the frame assembly. Order the shadow box and the glass to these measurements.

Several methods may be used for mounting items. Photographs and documents can be hinge-mounted, using linen framer's tape. Textile items, such as baptismal gowns and handkerchiefs, can be secured to the mounting board with small hand stitches. Many other items, such as earrings, lockets, and fishing poles, may also be secured with hand stitches. For inconspicuous stitches, use a thread that matches the item. Monofilament fishing line also works well for many items and is strong.

Lightweight items that cannot be stitched in place, such as plates, may be secured with clear silicone glue, available at hardware stores. This glue stays flexible and can be removed without damaging the item. Plastic clips designed for mounting items are available at framing stores in several sizes and styles to hold a variety of objects, including plates, pipes, coins, spoons, and fishing poles.

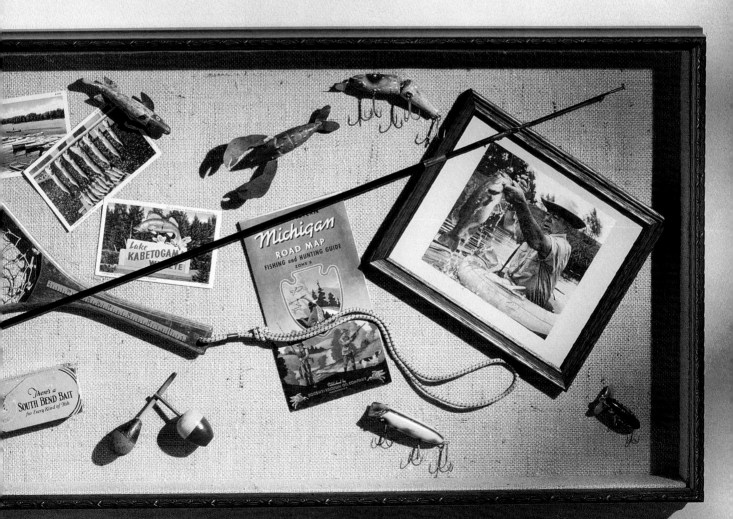

HOW TO MAKE A SHADOW BOX DISPLAY

MATERIALS

- Wooden shadow box.
- Natural-fiber fabric, such as 100 percent silk, linen, or cotton.
- ¼" (6 mm) acid-free foam-core board.
- Double-stick framer's tape, or ATG tape.
- Gummed linen framer's tape.
- Clear acrylic finish; paintbrush.
- Utility knife; cork-backed metal straightedge.
- Needle; thimble; thread; fishing line; clear silicone glue; or plastic mounting clips, such as Mighty Mounts™, as needed for mounting various items.

1 Seal unfinished wood of shadow box, using clear acrylic finish; allow to dry. Place glass in shadow box.

2 Mark strip of foam-core board ⅛" (3 mm) shorter and ⅜" (1 cm) shallower than inside top dimensions of the shadow box. Score repeatedly on marked lines, using utility knife and straightedge, until board is cut through. Repeat to cut strip for inside bottom.

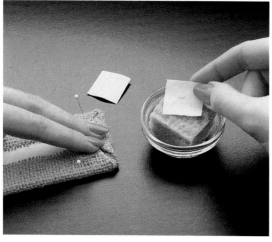

3 Cut fabric 2" (5 cm) larger than each strip of foam-core board. Secure double-stick framer's tape to the foam-core board along all the outer edges. Center foam-core board, tape side up, on wrong side of fabric. Wrap fabric firmly around the long sides; press in place onto tape.

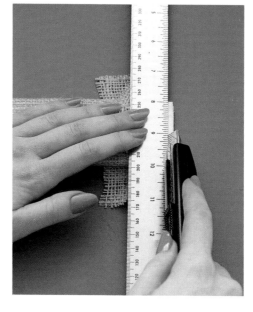

4 Wrap the fabric around ends, folding mitered corners; secure to tape. Secure the folded fabric at the corners, using moistened strips of linen framer's tape.

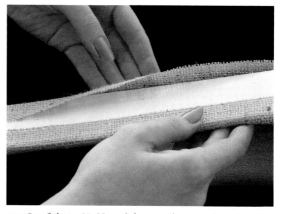

5 Position top and bottom pieces in frame; pieces should fit snugly without buckling. Repeat steps 2 to 4 for the side pieces. Check the fit of all pieces. If necessary, adjust size of pieces by peeling back fabric, then trimming the foam-core board and rewrapping it.

6 Cut mounting board ¼" (6 mm) smaller than the frame opening dimensions. Wrap mounting board with fabric as for side pieces. Check fit of mounting board; adjust, if necessary.

7 Remove the glass and clean it on both sides thoroughly, using a glass cleaner and a lint-free cloth. Reposition glass in frame. Cut strips of double-stick framer's tape; secure to back of each piece for sides of frame. Secure top and bottom pieces to frame, then side pieces.

8 Attach the items to the mounting board (below); attach photographs, if desired, with hinges made from gummed linen framer's tape.

9 Place mounting board in frame. Recheck the display and glass for lint or dust. Complete the frame assembly as on page 53, step 6.

TIPS FOR MOUNTING ITEMS IN A SHADOW BOX

Hand stitches. Arrange the item on mounting board. Determine several locations where article can be supported with small stitches. Thread a needle with monofilament fishing line or thread that matches item. Using threaded needle and thimble, secure item, taking about three stitches through mounting board at each support location. From back of board, tie the thread tails, and secure them to board with linen framer's tape.

Clear silicone glue. Secure any lightweight items with a bead of clear silicone glue. Allow the glue to cure for 24 hours before placing backing board into frame.

Plastic clips. Mark the location for holder. Punch hole to the back side of mounting board, using an awl. Insert the holder, and press speed nut into place. Trim the post a scant ⅛" (3 mm) from nut, using utility scissors or pruning shears.

DECORATIVE HANGING METHODS

Decorative hangers are used as nonfunctional accessories to provide interest to walls and artwork. Often used to link pictures together, decorative hangers can also be used to highlight a color, add texture, or visually increase the size of a wall grouping.

Cording adds elegance to traditional pictures. Accentuate the look, if desired, with tassels. For an Old World look, mount the cording high on the wall or at the ceiling level.

For a tailored accent, hang a picture using an ornate ring pull. Ring pulls are available in a variety of sizes and finishes at craft stores, hardware stores, and specialty woodworking stores. Hang the ring pulls from small nails or decorative hangers.

Decorative drawer pulls and ribbon can add a clean, tailored accent or a vintage look to a display, depending on the style of hardware and ribbon chosen. Select drawer pulls with wood thread screws, suitable for mounting to the wall. Other knobs intended for use with a bolt may be converted for use as decorative hangers by substituting a hanger bolt for the original bolt.

HOW TO HANG A PICTURE WITH CORDING

MATERIALS

- Cording; tassels, optional.
- Brad.
- Transparent or masking tape.

1 Hang picture. Fold the cording in half, and tie overhand knot about 2" (5 cm) from fold. Hand-stitch one or two tassels to knot, if desired. Secure the cording to the wall as desired, using brad; conceal the brad in knot.

2 Determine the desired drape of cording; pin-mark length at upper edge of frame. Remove cording from wall. Wrap tape around the cording about ½" (1.3 cm) below the pin marks; trim cording. Secure the cording to back of the frame with tape. Rehang the picture.

Drawer pulls and grosgrain ribbon
unite a trio of nature prints.

Ring pull and decorative hanger
add interest to a traditional print.

MORE IDEAS FOR DECORATIVE HANGERS

Chains, draped over decorative hangers, add interest to a mirror.

HOW TO HANG A PICTURE WITH A DRAWER PULL & RIBBON

MATERIALS

- Decorative drawer pull.
- Ribbon.
- Hanger bolt, if necessary, for securing drawer pull to wall.
- Drill and drill bit.
- Utility tape.

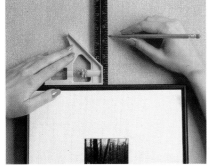

1 Hang the picture. Mark position on wall for drawer pull, taking care to center the mark above picture. Attach hanger bolt to drawer pull, if necessary. Secure drawer pull to wall; predrill hole, using drill bit slightly smaller than screw.

2 Drape the ribbon over the drawer pull. Pin-mark the length of ribbon at upper edge of frame, keeping the ribbon taut.

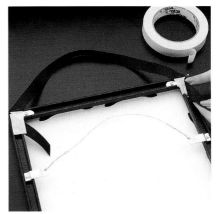

3 Secure ribbon to back of frame with tape, aligning pin marks to upper edge of frame. Rehang picture.

Ribbon, ring pull, and drawer pull are combined to add height and prominence to a picture.

Plaster relief is paired with a tapestry ribbon to create a decorative hanger.

HOW TO HANG A PICTURE WITH A RING PULL

MATERIALS

- Decorative ring pull.
- Decorative hanger or brass nail.
- Awl.
- Drill and drill bit.

1 Mark the center of frame at upper edge, using awl. Predrill hole, using drill bit slightly smaller than the ring pull screw.

2 Secure the ring pull to the frame. Hang the picture. Mark location for nail or decorative hanger, and tap into position.

INDEX

Creative Publishing international, Inc.
offers a variety of how-to books. For infor-
mation write:
    Creative Publishing international, Inc.
    Subscriber Books
    5900 Green Oak Drive
    Minnetonka, MN 55343